16 weeks of fun and easy ways to
and mindfulness to your school c

Classroom
YOGA
IN 10 MINUTES A DAY

Written by Giselle Shardlow

KIDS
YOGA
STORIES

kidsyogastories.com

Kids Yoga Stories
Boston, MA
www.kidsyogastories.com
www.amazon.com/author/giselleshardlow
Email us at **info@kidsyogastories.com**.

What do you think? Let us know what you think of *Classroom Yoga in 10 Minutes a Day* at **feedback@kidsyogastories.com**.

Welcome to your
Classroom Yoga
IN 10 MINUTES A DAY

This classroom yoga resource is for kids yoga teachers, parents, caregivers, and health practitioners looking for fun, simple ways to add yoga to your school curriculum.

To spark your imagination, there are specific activities for each day of the week, themed under:

- Mindful Mondays
- Twisty Tuesdays
- Wind-Down Wednesdays
- Theme Thursdays
- Fun Fridays

Use these five-to-ten-minute ideas as a springboard and feel free to add other age-appropriate theme-related yoga poses, songs, breathing techniques, relaxation stories, meditations, art projects, and field trips.

To make your classroom yoga experience as successful as possible, try these ideas:

- Print out each week's section beforehand to get familiar with the activities.
- Create a ritual before each yoga session (for example, sit in a circle and sing a yoga song).
- Focus on having fun with movement, not on practicing perfectly aligned poses.
- Engage the children.
- Follow their passions and interests.
- Create authentic, meaningful experiences.

- Cater to their energy levels and different learning styles.

- Be creative and enjoy yourself—the kids will notice your enthusiasm.

- Encourage children to make up their own yoga and mindfulness activities.

- Brainstorm other yoga poses that fit the various topics.

- Wear comfortable clothing and practice on a non-slip surface.

- Make safety a top priority—clear the space of obstacles and be safe with your bodies.

- Encourage the children to share their yoga experiences with their families and friends.

- End each week by reflecting on their favorite poses, meditations, and games.

Get your children learning, moving, and having fun in the classroom with these fun and easy yoga activities in 10 minutes a day!

Classroom Yoga
IN 10 MINUTES A DAY
Where to Start

1. Print out (or view on your device) the Weekly Schedule on the following pages.

2. Print out (or view) each week's packet, which includes:

   • List of the daily activities

   • Printables of the daily activities

3. Extend any activity that the children are particularly interested in or do it again on another day.

4. Celebrate the miracles along the way. Allow space to talk about what they like about the yoga, mindfulness, and meditation activities and reflect on what's working and how you could improve the experiences.

5. If you miss a day, don't worry; just pick up where you left off, then use the activities you missed on the weekend or double-up on some days. The schedule is meant to be flexible to suit your needs.

Classroom Yoga
IN 10 MINUTES A DAY

Weekly Schedule

Week One (page 1)

MINDFUL MONDAY	TWISTY TUESDAY	WIND-DOWN WEDNESDAY	THEME THURSDAY	FUN FRIDAY
Pause Breath	Tree Pose like a Tree	Owl Coloring Page	Beginning Yoga Poster	Roll the Pose Game

Week Two (page 9)

MINDFUL MONDAY	TWISTY TUESDAY	WIND-DOWN WEDNESDAY	THEME THURSDAY	FUN FRIDAY
Calm Meditation	Cat Pose in a Chair	Cat-Cow Pose Coloring Pages	Pets Yoga Poster	Pose Match Game

Week Three (page 19)

MINDFUL MONDAY	TWISTY TUESDAY	WIND-DOWN WEDNESDAY	THEME THURSDAY	FUN FRIDAY
Positive Affirmation Cards	Horse Stance like a Horse	Stop, Listen, What Do You Hear?	Unicorn Yoga Poster	Yogi Says Game

Week Four (page 27)

MINDFUL MONDAY	TWISTY TUESDAY	WIND-DOWN WEDNESDAY	THEME THURSDAY	FUN FRIDAY
Deep Belly Breath	Child's Pose in a Chair	Garden Gnome Flower Pose Coloring Page	Growth Mindset Yoga Poster	Spin the Pose Game

Classroom Yoga
IN 10 MINUTES A DAY

Weekly Schedule
(continued)

Week Five (page 35)				
MINDFUL MONDAY	TWISTY TUESDAY	WIND-DOWN WEDNESDAY	THEME THURSDAY	FUN FRIDAY
Gratitude Meditation	Standing Forward Bend like a Jelly	Turtle Coloring Page	Gratitude Yoga Poster	Yoga Yahtzee Game

Week Six (page 45)				
MINDFUL MONDAY	TWISTY TUESDAY	WIND-DOWN WEDNESDAY	THEME THURSDAY	FUN FRIDAY
Positive Affirmation Cards	Seated Twist Pose in a Chair	Resting Pose Coloring Page	Balancing Yoga Poster	Hold that Pose Game

Week Seven (page 53)				
MINDFUL MONDAY	TWISTY TUESDAY	WIND-DOWN WEDNESDAY	THEME THURSDAY	FUN FRIDAY
Figure 8 Breath	Boat Pose like a Boat	The Cloud Show	Sloth Yoga Poster	Strike a Pose Game

Week Eight (page 61)				
MINDFUL MONDAY	TWISTY TUESDAY	WIND-DOWN WEDNESDAY	THEME THURSDAY	FUN FRIDAY
Creativity Meditation	Pigeon Pose in a Chair	Garden Gnome Tree Pose Coloring Page	Cowboy and Cowgirl Partner Yoga Poster	Pick a Pose Stick Game

Classroom Yoga
IN 10 MINUTES A DAY

Weekly Schedule
(continued)

Week Nine (page 69)				
MINDFUL MONDAY	TWISTY TUESDAY	WIND-DOWN WEDNESDAY	THEME THURSDAY	FUN FRIDAY
Positive Affirmation Cards	Eagle Pose like an Eagle	Butterfly Coloring Page	Be My Best Yoga Poster	Yoga Pose Spinner Game

Week Ten (page 77)				
MINDFUL MONDAY	TWISTY TUESDAY	WIND-DOWN WEDNESDAY	THEME THURSDAY	FUN FRIDAY
Candle Breath	Wide-Legged Forward Bend in a Chair	Eagle Pose Coloring Page	Winter Activities Yoga Poster	What Time Is It, Yogi?

Week Eleven (page 85)				
MINDFUL MONDAY	TWISTY TUESDAY	WIND-DOWN WEDNESDAY	THEME THURSDAY	FUN FRIDAY
Happiness Meditation	Warrior 2 Pose like a Surfer	Rainstorm Hands	Core Yoga Poster	I'm Going to Yoga Class Game

Week Twelve (page 93)				
MINDFUL MONDAY	TWISTY TUESDAY	WIND-DOWN WEDNESDAY	THEME THURSDAY	FUN FRIDAY
Positive Affirmation Cards	Downward-Facing Dog Pose in a Chair	Garden Gnome Seated Cat Pose Coloring Page	Superhero Partner Yoga Poster	Build the Poses Game

Classroom Yoga
IN 10 MINUTES A DAY

Weekly Schedule
(continued)

Week Thirteen (page 101)

MINDFUL MONDAY	TWISTY TUESDAY	WIND-DOWN WEDNESDAY	THEME THURSDAY	FUN FRIDAY
Take 5 Breath	Dancer's Pose like a Dancer	Peacock Coloring Page	Empathy Partner Yoga Poster	Spell Your Pose Flow Game

Week Fourteen (page 109)

MINDFUL MONDAY	TWISTY TUESDAY	WIND-DOWN WEDNESDAY	THEME THURSDAY	FUN FRIDAY
Power Breath	Side Bend in a Chair	Cobbler's Pose Coloring Page	Energizing Yoga Poster	Odd or Even Poses Game

Week Fifteen (page 117)

MINDFUL MONDAY	TWISTY TUESDAY	WIND-DOWN WEDNESDAY	THEME THURSDAY	FUN FRIDAY
Positive Affirmation Cards	Extended Side Angle Pose like a Windsurfer	The Great Outdoors	Yoga Inversions Poster	Follow the Yogi Game

Week Sixteen (page 125)

MINDFUL MONDAY	TWISTY TUESDAY	WIND-DOWN WEDNESDAY	THEME THURSDAY	FUN FRIDAY
Hope Meditation	Triangle Forward Bend in a Chair	Garden Gnome Gate Pose Coloring Page	Garden Gnome Partner Yoga Poster	Yoga Board Game

Classroom Yoga
IN 10 MINUTES A DAY
Week One

MINDFUL MONDAY

Pause Breath

Take a moment to practice Pause Breath throughout the day. Model it for your children and talk about the benefits of taking a moment to take a deep breath.

TWISTY TUESDAY

Tree Pose

Try swaying like a tree in the breeze in Tree Pose. Hold for a few moments on one side and then repeat on the other side.

WIND-DOWN WEDNESDAY

Owl Coloring Page

Get out your colored pencils or crayons to spend some relaxing time coloring in the owl. Put on some gentle music and talk about owls or other forest animals.

THEME THURSDAY

Beginner Yoga Poster

Try these basic yoga poses, following the sequence listed on the poster. Try to hold each pose for a few breaths to allow your body to get familiar with the poses.

FUN FRIDAY

Roll the Pose Game

Grab a partner and get out some dice to play this fun Roll the Pose game. Pick six poses to write or draw in the squares on the template provided, roll the dice, and practice the associated pose.

Pause Breath

How to practice Pause Breath

Stop what you're doing and take a moment to pause. Place a hand on your chest, close your eyes if that's comfortable, and take a few deep breaths. Feel the rise and fall of your hand on your chest. Do this deep belly breathing for a minute to help slow down your mind and body.

KIDS
YOGA
STORIES

kidsyogastories.com
© Kids Yoga Stories

Sway like a tree in the breeze

TREE POSE

Tree Pose

Stand on one leg. Bend the knee of the leg you are not standing on, place the sole of your foot on the opposite inner thigh or calf (just not on your knee), and balance. Switch sides and repeat the steps. Pretend to **sway like a tree in the breeze**.

kidsyogastories.com

BEGINNER YOGA

Hero Pose
VIRASANA

Cat-Cow Pose Flow
BITILASANA MARJARYASANA

Downward-Facing Dog Pose
ADHO MUKHA SVANASANA

Child's Pose
BALASANA

Resting Pose
SAVASANA

BEGINNER YOGA

1. Hero Pose (Virasana)

How to practice Hero Pose (Virasana): Come to rest upright on your heels with your palms resting on your knees. Close your eyes, if that's comfortable. Take a few deep breaths and relax.

2. Cat-Cow Pose Flow (Bitilasana Marjaryasana)

How to practice Cat-Cow Pose Flow (Bitilasana Marjaryasana): Come to an all-fours position, tuck your chin into your chest, and round your back into Cat Pose. Then look up, open your chest, and arch your back in a Cow Pose. Repeat this Cat-Cow flow a few times to warm up your spine.

3. Downward-Facing Dog Pose (Adho Mukha Svanasana)

How to practice Downward-Facing Dog Pose (Adho Mukha Svanasana): Lift your knees to an upside-down V shape, with your buttocks up in the air. Ensure that your palms are flat on the ground with your fingers splayed out. Your spine is long, and you can look between your legs. Breathe and relax.

4. Child's Pose (Balasana)

How to practice Child's Pose (Balasana): Drop your knees and sit back on your heels. Slowly bring your forehead down to rest on the floor in front of your knees, rest your arms down alongside your body, and take a few deep breaths.

5. Resting Pose (Savasana)

How to practice Resting Pose (Savasana): Lie on your back with your arms and legs stretched out. Close your eyes. Breathe and rest.

Roll the Pose

What you need: Roll the Pose gameboard and 1 die

HOW TO PLAY:

1. Draw the name of a pose or draw a pose in each of the boxes numbered 1 to 6.

2. Taking turns, players roll the die and then practice the pose associated with their number.

3. Each player could take a turn by themselves or all players could play at the same time.

4. Play continues for a selected amount of time.

SAMPLE GAME

1	2
Tree Pose	Cat Pose
3	**4**
Downward-Facing Dog Pose	Boat Pose
5	**6**
Cobbler's Pose	Chair Pose

kidsyogastories.com
© Kids Yoga Stories

Roll the Pose

1	2
3	4
5	6

KIDS YOGA STORIES

Classroom Yoga
IN 10 MINUTES A DAY
Week Two

MINDFUL MONDAY

Calm Meditation

Take a few minutes to read aloud the Calm Meditation (body scan). Feel free to color the matching coloring page as you listen.

Twisty Tuesday

Cat Pose in a Chair

Try this chair yoga pose by sitting with your feet flat on the ground. Then round your back and tuck your chin into your chest. Use this as a time to reboot and refocus.

WIND-DOWN WEDNESDAY

Cat-Cow Pose Coloring Pages

Get out your colored pencils or crayons to spend some relaxing time coloring in the cat and cow poses. Put on some gentle music and maybe talk about what you might find at a farm.

THEME THURSDAY

Pets Yoga Poster

Try these pet yoga poses, following the sequence listed on the poster. Try to hold each pose for a few breaths, and you could even make the sounds of each animal.

FUN FRIDAY

Pose Match Game

Get out one die, a deck of yoga cards, and sticky notes to play this yoga dice game. Feel free to make your own variations of the game.

Calm

Lie down comfortably on your back with your arms and legs stretched out.

Be still for a moment, taking in a few deep breaths.

Close your eyes and think about melting into the ground.

Let go of any thoughts from your day. Breathe and relax.

Now, following my voice, you're going to bring your attention to different parts of your body.

For example, when I say "feet," you're going to bring your attention to your feet and simply relax them.

Don't worry about getting it right. Just listen to my voice.

Let's begin. First, bring your attention to your feet. Relax your feet. Then, bring your attention to your lower legs. Relax your lower legs. Next, your knees. Your upper legs. Your belly. And your chest.

Next, think about your hands. Relax your hands. Then your elbows. Then your arms. Then your shoulders.

Now, think about your face. Relax your face. Then your chin. Your mouth. Your nose. Your eyes. And your head.

Think about the different parts of your body. Does any part of it need a little extra love today?

Take in a few deep breaths. As you inhale, think, "I am strong." As you exhale, think, "I am calm."

Continue like that for a few deep breaths, alternating between thoughts of "I am strong," and "I am calm."

Know that you are safe and cared for. Breathe and relax. Let it go.

When you are ready, open your eyes.

KIDS YOGA STORIES

kidsyogastories.com
© Kids Yoga Stories

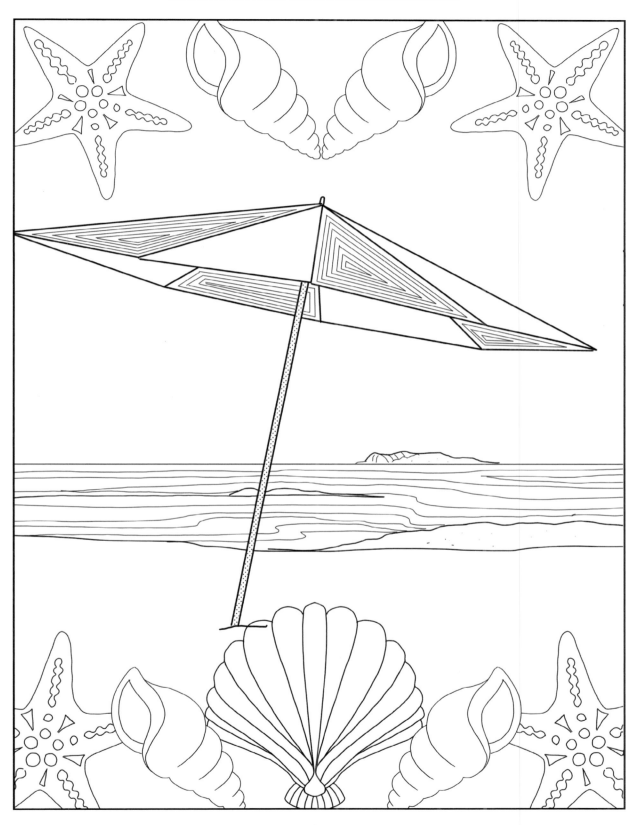

Cat Pose

How to practice Cat Pose

From a sitting position with your feet flat on the ground, round your back and tuck your chin into your chest, stretching your back.

PETS YOGA

 I am a puppy.
DOWNWARD-FACING DOG POSE

 I am a goldfish.
LOCUST POSE

 I am a kitten.
CAT POSE

 I am a bunny.
HARE POSE

 I am a hamster.
HAPPY BABY POSE

PETS YOGA

1. Pretend to be a puppy.

How to practice Downward-Facing Dog Pose: Step back to your hands and feet in an upside-down V shape, with your buttocks up in the air. Pretend to be a puppy playing in the backyard.

2. Pretend to be a goldfish.

How to practice Locust Pose: Lie on your tummy, lift your chest and shoulders, and look up. Pretend to be goldfish swimming around a fish tank.

3. Pretend to be a kitten.

How to practice Cat Pose: On all fours, round your back and tuck your chin into your chest. Pretend to be a kitten taking a stretch after a nap.

4. Pretend to be a bunny.

How to practice Hare Pose: Come to sitting on your heels in a Hero Pose. Slowly place your head out in front of you on the ground. Take your hands back alongside your body. Then, lift up your buttocks, being careful to not put too much pressure on your head. Pretend to be a bunny ready for its snack.

5. Pretend to be a hamster.

How to practice Happy Baby Pose: Lie on your back with your chin tucked in, hug your knees into your chest, then grab the outer parts of each foot—right foot in right hand and left foot in left hand. Pretend to be a hamster on its back.

Pose Match

WHAT YOU NEED:	die, deck of yoga cards (only the pose cards), and sticky notes
MATH SKILLS:	number recognition, matching
PLAYERS:	1 or more

HOW TO PLAY:

1. Grab a die.

2. Write the numbers 1 through 6 on sticky notes, one note for each number. You can write both the numeral and the number symbol found on dice, if you like.

3. Have your child pick out six pose cards from the deck.

4. Stick a numbered note on each pose card. You can put the yoga poses in a logical yoga flow with standing poses first, followed by floor poses and resting poses.

5. Roll the die and practice the yoga pose associated with that number.

VARIATIONS:

*   *Change up the game by simply sticking the numbered sticky notes on different yoga cards for a second round.*

*   *Use two dice and twelve pose cards. Roll the dice and add the two numbers together then practice the pose associated with the number.*

   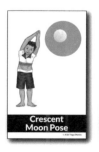  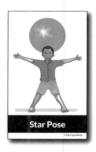

Mountain Pose | Extended Mountain Pose | Dolphin Plank Pose | Crescent Moon Pose | Swan Pose | Star Pose

1   2   3   4   5   6

Classroom Yoga
IN 10 MINUTES A DAY
Week Three

MINDFUL MONDAY

Positive Affirmation Cards (proud, positive, peaceful)
Color the three affirmation cards with colored pencils or crayons, or feel free to use a different medium. Talk about the words and what they mean to you.

Twisty Tuesday

Horse Stance
Stand strong like a horse in Horse Stance. Hold for a few moments and then try to bend your legs even more to a deeper squat, while keeping a straight spine. Feel proud and steady.

WIND-DOWN WEDNESDAY

Stop, Listen, What Do You Hear?
Take a moment to practice this mindfulness activity by listening to sounds far away, then nearby, and then inside you. This will help bring you to the present moment.

THEME THURSDAY

Unicorn Yoga Poster
Try these unicorn yoga poses, following the sequence listed on the poster. Say the matching positive statement and hold each pose for a few breaths.

FUN FRIDAY

Yogi Says Game
Following the game instructions, pick a "yogi" to lead the group through a series of yoga poses. Listen carefully so you don't get out!

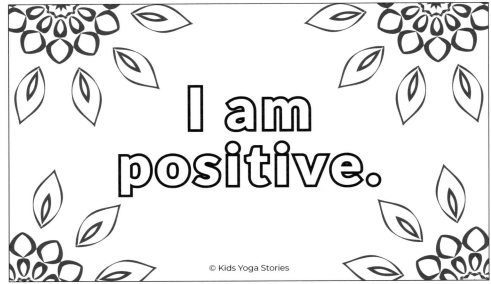

Stand strong like a horse

HORSE STANCE

Horse Stance

Stand with your legs apart, feet facing slightly outward. Bend your knees and stand firm. Pretend to **stand strong like a horse**.

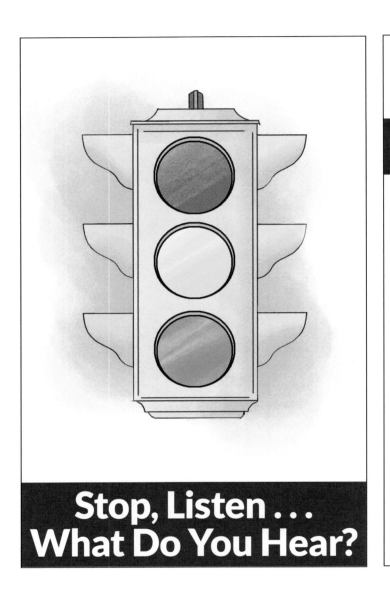

Stop, Listen . . .
What Do You Hear?

Stop, Listen . . .
What Do You Hear?

Stop for a moment, close your eyes, and listen for the sounds around you. Listen for two faraway sounds, two nearby sounds, then two sounds right beside or inside you.

KIDS YOGA STORIES

kidsyogastories.com
© Kids Yoga Stories

UNICORN YOGA

I am a peaceful unicorn.
EASY POSE

I am a proud unicorn.
WARRIOR 1 POSE

I am a confident unicorn.
WARRIOR 2 POSE

I am a graceful unicorn.
REVERSE WARRIOR POSE

I am a kind unicorn.
TREE POSE

UNICORN YOGA

1. I am a peaceful unicorn.

How to practice Easy Pose: Sit cross-legged and rest your palms on your knees. Close your eyes if you are comfortable doing so. Pretend to be a peaceful unicorn. Take a few deep breaths and relax your body.

2. I am a proud unicorn.

How to practice Warrior 1 Pose: Step one foot back, angling your toes slightly outward, and bend your front knee. Reach both arms up overhead. Switch sides and repeat the steps. Pretend to be a proud unicorn.

3. I am a confident unicorn.

How to practice Warrior 2 Pose: From Warrior 1, reach both arms out to the sides and look over your front fingertips. Make sure your front knee is bent forward. Pretend to be a confident unicorn. Switch sides and repeat the steps.

4. I am a graceful unicorn.

How to practice Reverse Warrior Pose: From standing position, step your left foot back, angling your toes slightly outward. Raise your arms parallel to the ground, bringing your right hand forward and your left to the back. Bend your front knee and look forward. Flip your right palm up to the sky, tilt your torso backward, and rest your left hand on your left thigh. Look up at your extended hand, open your chest, and keep your spine long and straight. Pretend to be a graceful unicorn. Come back to center and repeat on the other side.

5. I am a kind unicorn.

How to practice Tree Pose: Stand on one leg. Bend the knee of the leg you are not standing on, place the sole of your foot on the opposite inner thigh or calf (just not on your knee), and balance. Pretend to be a kind unicorn. Switch sides and repeat the steps.

KIDS
YOGA
STORIES

kidsyogastories.com
© Kids Yoga Stories

Yogi Says

Adapted from Simons Says, this game is a fun choice for even the youngest players, and it is flexible enough to fill shorter or longer breaks.

What you need: yoga pose cards (optional)

HOW TO PLAY:

1. One child is picked to be the "yogi."

2. The yogi calls out various yoga poses for the players to then follow along. For example, "Yogi says, 'Practice Tree Pose'" or "Yogi says, 'Practice Warrior 1 Pose.'"

3. At some point, the yogi will not start the instruction with "Yogi says, 'Practice...'" and will simply say "Practice..." Any player who follows that instruction is eliminated from the game by sitting down or stepping to the side.

4. The game continues until all the players are out of the game.

5. Then another yogi is chosen and play continues.

VARIATIONS:

- *Choose not to actually eliminate any players, but just continue the game.*

- *The yogi could pick a pose from a yoga pose card deck to make it easier to choose the pose.*

- *Give the yogi a selection of yoga pose cards to choose from if there are specific poses that they were intending to focus on (ex. balancing, core, standing, thematic).*

Classroom Yoga
IN 10 MINUTES A DAY
Week Four

MINDFUL MONDAY

Deep Belly Breath

Take a moment to practice Deep Belly Breath throughout the day. Model it for your children and talk about the benefits of taking a moment to take a deep breath.

Twisty Tuesday

Child's Pose in a Chair

Try this chair yoga pose during a subject change throughout the day, when you return from recess and need to refocus, or if you just need a brain break.

WIND-DOWN WEDNESDAY

Garden Gnome Flower Pose Coloring Page

Get out your colored pencils or crayons to spend some relaxing time coloring in the garden gnomes. Put on some gentle music and talk about flowers and gardens. Try the pose with a partner.

THEME THURSDAY

Growth Mindset Yoga Poster

Try these growth mindset yoga poses, following the sequence listed on the poster. Say the matching positive statement and hold each pose for a few breaths.

FUN FRIDAY

Spin the Pose Game

Following the game instructions, get out a spinner (or paperclip) and arrange your yoga pose cards around in a circle. Spin the spinner and practice the pose.

27

Deep Belly Breath

How to practice Deep Belly Breath

Place your right hand on your belly and your left hand on your chest. Take a deep breath in for four counts then exhale through your nose for four counts, with your lips closed. Feel the rise and fall of your chest and belly. If you're on your back, you could place an object, like a stuffed animal, on your stomach to help you feel (and see) the rise and fall of your belly. Do this deep belly breathing for a few minutes.

KIDS YOGA STORIES

kidsyogastories.com

Child's Pose

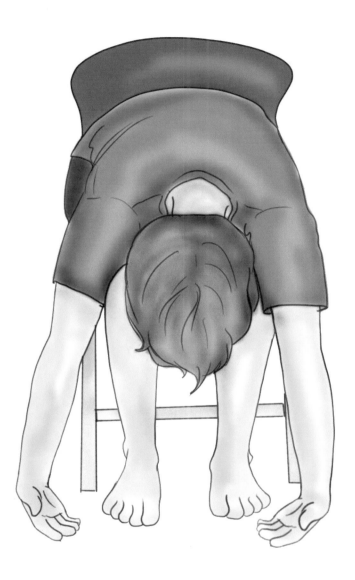

How to practice Child's Pose

Sit back on your chair, slowly bend your upper body to rest on your thighs, rest your arms down towards the floor, and take a few deep breaths.

KIDS
YOGA
STORIES

kidsyogastories.com
© Kids Yoga Stories

Flower Pose

KIDS
YOGA
STORIES

kidsyogastories.com
© Kids Yoga Stories

GROWTH MINDSET YOGA

I am hardworking.
WARRIOR 1 POSE

I am creative.
DANCER'S POSE

I am focused.
CHAIR POSE

I am open-minded.
LUNGE POSE

I am curious.
DOWNWARD-FACING DOG POSE

GROWTH MINDSET YOGA

1. I am hardworking.

How to practice Warrior 1 Pose: Stand tall with legs hip-width apart, feet facing forward, and straighten your arms alongside your body. Step one foot back, angling it slightly outward. Bend your front knee, bring your arms straight up toward the sky, and look up. Imagine working hard through a problem and embracing challenges. Say, "I am hardworking." Repeat on the other side.

2. I am creative.

How to practice Dancer's Pose: Stand tall in Mountain Pose. Then stand on your right leg, reach your left leg out behind you, and place the outside of your left foot into your left hand. Bend your torso forward, with your right arm out in front for balance, and arch your leg up behind you. Imagine using your creativity to face setbacks in a different way. Say, "I am creative." Switch sides and repeat the steps.

3. I am focused.

How to practice Chair Pose: Stand tall in Mountain Pose with your feet hip-width apart, bend your knees, and keep a straight spine. Take your straight arms out in front of you at a forty-five-degree angle. Focus on giving your best effort to hold this difficult pose as long as you can. Think of when you could use focus and effort to master a task in real life. Say, "I am focused."

4. I am open-minded.

How to practice Lunge Pose: From Downward-Facing Dog Pose, step your right foot forward to rest just inside your right hand. Keep a flat back and open your chest. Imagine being open-minded enough to listen and learn from someone giving you constructive criticism. Say, "I am open-minded." Switch sides and repeat the steps.

5. I am curious.

How to practice Downward-Facing Dog Pose: Step back to your hands and feet in an upside-down V shape, with your buttocks up in the air. Think of ways that people around you have experienced success. Be curious and inspired by their successes. Say, "I am curious."

KIDS YOGA STORIES

kidsyogastories.com
© Kids Yoga Stories

Spin the Pose

WHAT YOU NEED:	pose cards from a deck of yoga cards, spinner, sticky note
PLAYERS:	1 or more

HOW TO PLAY:

1. Grab the pose cards.

2. Place a sticky note under one corner of a fidget spinner to act as a pointer.

3. Pick out six pose cards and arrange them in a circle around the spinner.

4. You might want to use Blu Tack or something similar on the bottom of the spinner's center to make sure it doesn't spin away.

5. Spin the spinner then practice the pose that the pointer lands on.

6. Continue to play with multiple players or solo, for as long as you'd like.

VARIATIONS:

- *Change the pose cards after a few rounds and play again.*

- *Use partner pose cards and practice in pairs.*

- *Use chair yoga or breathing exercise cards.*

- *Put three yoga cards on top of each other, then practice that 3-pose flow when you land on that pile.*

- *Place the yoga cards upside down so the pose is a surprise.*

Classroom Yoga
IN 10 MINUTES A DAY
Week Five

MINDFUL MONDAY

Gratitude Meditation

Take a few minutes to read aloud the Gratitude Meditation. Feel free to color the matching coloring page as you listen.

Twisty Tuesday

Standing Forward Bend

Dangle your tentacles like a jelly in Standing Forward Bend. Hold for a few moments and imagine yourself flowing through the ocean waters.

WIND-DOWN WEDNESDAY

Turtle Coloring Page

Get out your colored pencils or crayons to spend some relaxing time coloring in the turtle. Put on some gentle music and maybe talk about the animals you might find in the ocean.

THEME THURSDAY

Gratitude Yoga Poster

Try these gratitude yoga poses, following the sequence listed on the poster. Say the matching statement and hold each pose for a few breaths.

FUN FRIDAY

Yoga Yahtzee

Following the game instructions, get out your gameboard template and draw or write a different yoga poses next to each number. Roll the dice, put a counter on that pose, and then practice the pose.

Gratitude

Close your eyes and tune in to the sound of your breath.

Take a deep breath in then exhale slowly for three to five counts.

On your next exhale, think, "I am grateful for myself."

On the next exhale, think, "I am grateful to my family."

Then on the next exhale, think, "I am grateful to my friends."

Continue like this, sending gratitude to the animals, the forest, the ocean, your neighbors, your community, or whatever is meaningful to you.

Lastly, think, "I am grateful for the whole world. May we all be happy and free."

Finish your gratitude meditation by coming back to breathing naturally.

When you are ready, open your eyes.

Dangle your tentacles like a jellyfish
STANDING FORWARD BEND

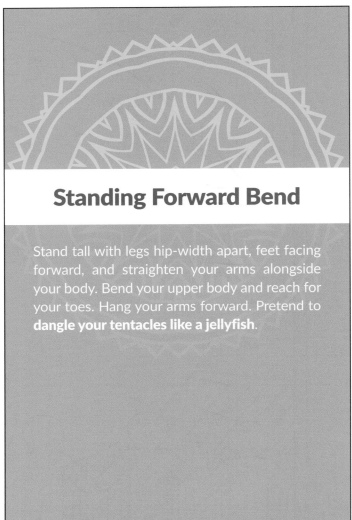

Standing Forward Bend

Stand tall with legs hip-width apart, feet facing forward, and straighten your arms alongside your body. Bend your upper body and reach for your toes. Hang your arms forward. Pretend to **dangle your tentacles like a jellyfish**.

kidsyogastories.com
© Kids Yoga Stories

GRATITUDE YOGA
I am grateful for...

Trees that provide us with oxygen.
TREE POSE

Stars to make wishes upon.
STAR POSE

Rain clouds that bring us fresh water.
STANDING FORWARD BEND

Bees that pollinate crops.
HERO POSE

The earth and its animals, people, and places.
CHILD'S POSE

KIDS YOGA STORIES

kidsyogastories.com
© Kids Yoga Stories

40

GRATITUDE YOGA
I am grateful for...

1. Trees that provide us with oxygen.

How to practice Tree Pose: Stand on one leg. Bend the knee of the leg you are not standing on, place the sole of your foot on the opposite inner thigh or calf (just not on your knee), and balance. Pretend to be a tree making oxygen. Switch sides and repeat the steps.

2. Stars to make wishes upon.

How to practice Star Pose: From a standing position, step your feet out wide. Lift both arms out to your sides and above your head, with your fingers spread out. Pretend to be a shooting star in the night sky.

3. Rain clouds that bring us fresh water.

How to practice Standing Forward Bend: From Mountain Pose, bend your upper body, keep a straight spine, and reach for your toes. Pretend to be a cloud and that your arms are the falling rain.

4. Bees that pollinate crops.

How to practice Hero Pose: Come to rest upright on your heels with your palms resting on your knees. Pretend to be a bee by making a buzzing sound and flapping your hands like the wings of a bee.

5. The earth and its animals, people, and places.

How to practice Child's Pose: Sit on your heels, slowly bring your forehead down to rest on the floor in front of your knees, rest your arms down alongside your body, and take a few deep breaths. Pretend to be the earth.

Yoga Yahtzee

What you need:	Yoga Yahtzee gameboard, 2 dice, and counters

HOW TO PLAY:

1. Get out your Yoga Yahtzee gameboard template or draw your own.

2. Write or draw a different yoga pose next to each number.

3. The first player rolls the two dice and adds them together to make a sum. Then they place a counter on that number and practice the matching yoga pose.

4. The second player takes a turn, doing the same as the first player.

5. Play continues until one of the players fills up their Yoga Yahtzee board and is the winner.

SAMPLE GAME

2 Crescent Lunge	2 Triangle Forward Bend
3 Downhill Skier	3 Puppy Pose
4 Crescent Moon	4 Lunge Pose
5 Humble Warrior	5 Crescent Lunge
6 Lunge Pose	6 Humble Warrior
7 Star Pose	7 Downhill Skier
8 Puppy Pose	8 Extended Cat
9 Reverse Plank Pose	9 Standing Chest Stretch
10 Standing Chest Stretch	10 Crescent Moon
11 Extended Cat	11 Reverse Plank Pose
12 Triangle Forward Bend	12 Star Pose

Yoga Yahtzee

2		2	
3		3	
4		4	
5		5	
6		6	
7		7	
8		8	
9		9	
10		10	
11		11	
12		12	

Classroom Yoga
IN 10 MINUTES A DAY
Week Six

MINDFUL MONDAY

Positive Affirmation Cards (calm, caring, confident)
Color the three affirmation cards with colored pencils or crayons, or feel free to use a different medium. Talk about the words and what they mean to you.

Twisty Tuesday

Seated Twist Pose in a Chair
Try this chair yoga pose during a subject change throughout the day, when you return from recess and need to refocus, or if you just need a brain break.

WIND-DOWN WEDNESDAY

Resting Pose Coloring Page
Get out your colored pencils or crayons to spend some relaxing time coloring in the resting pose page. Put on some gentle music and maybe talk about ways that you like to relax and chill out.

THEME THURSDAY

Balancing Yoga Poster
Try these balancing yoga poses, following the sequence listed on the poster. Try to hold each pose for as long as you can – even up to a minute long.

FUN FRIDAY

Hold That Pose Game
Following the game instructions, get out a die and deck of yoga pose cards. Grab a partner, pick a pose, roll the die, and have fun holding various poses.

I am calm.

© Kids Yoga Stories

I am caring.

© Kids Yoga Stories

I am confident.

© Kids Yoga Stories

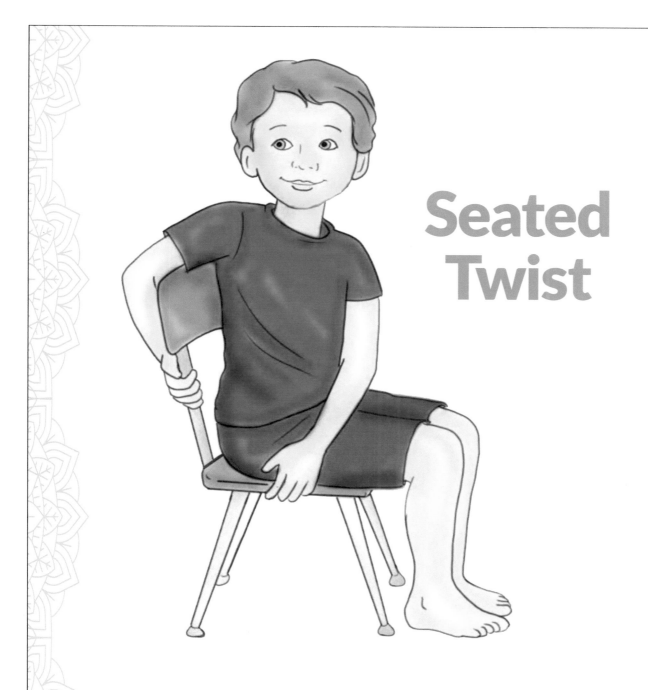

Seated Twist

How to practice Seated Twist

Sit upright in your chair. Check that your spine is straight and your feet are flat on the ground. Twist your upper body to the right. Take your left hand to your right thigh (or knee) and your right hand back behind the chair. Repeat on the other side.

kidsyogastories.com
© Kids Yoga Stories

BALANCING YOGA

Tree Pose

Dancer's Pose

Extended Hand-to-Big-Toe Pose

Warrior 3 Pose

Crescent Lunge

BALANCING YOGA

1. Tree Pose

How to practice Tree Pose: Stand on one leg. Bend the knee of the leg you are not standing on, place the sole of your foot on the opposite inner thigh or calf (just not on your knee), and balance. Switch sides and repeat the steps.

2. Dancer's Pose

How to practice Dancer's Pose: Stand tall in Mountain Pose. Then stand on your right leg, reach your left leg out behind you, and place the outside of your left foot into your left hand. Bend your torso forward, with your right arm out in front for balance, and arch your leg up behind you. Switch sides and repeat the steps.

3. Extended Hand-to-Big-Toe Pose

How to practice Extended Hand-to-Big-Toe Pose: From a standing position, bend your right knee toward your chest. Grab your right big toe with your right hand and place your left hand on your left hip. Extend your right leg out to the side, straightening the leg as much as possible. Hold this pose for a few breaths then bring your leg down slowly. Switch sides and repeat the steps.

4. Warrior 3 Pose

How to practice Warrior 3 Pose: Stand on one leg. Extend the other leg behind you, flexing your foot. Bend your torso forward and take your arms back alongside your body. Switch sides and repeat the steps.

5. Crescent Lunge

How to practice Crescent Lunge: From a standing position, step your right foot back into a lunge with your left foot directly over your left knee and a straight back leg. Inhale and take your parallel arms straight up overhead. Open your chest, look up, and take a few deep breaths. Switch sides and repeat the steps.

Hold that Pose

WHAT YOU NEED:	die, deck of yoga cards (only the pose cards)
MATH SKILLS:	number recognition, counting
PLAYERS:	1 or more

HOW TO PLAY:

1. Place a deck of yoga cards facedown in front of players.

2. The first player rolls the die and takes the top yoga pose card from the pile.

3. The player practices that pose, while counting to the number on the die. For example, the player rolls a three and picks a Tree Pose. He balances in Tree Pose while counting "1 – 2 – 3."

4. Play continues for a certain amount of time or until the deck is finished.

VARIATIONS:

- *Play with more than two players. Have everyone practice the pose and count along with a leader.*

- *Use a numbered deck of cards instead of dice for higher numbers.*

Classroom Yoga
IN 10 MINUTES A DAY
Week Seven

MINDFUL MONDAY

Figure 8 Breath
Take a moment to practice Figure 8 Breath throughout the day. Model it for your children and talk about the benefits of taking a moment to take a deep breath.

Twisty Tuesday

Boat Pose
Row down the river in a boat while practicing Boat Pose. Hold for a few moments to activate your core strength. You could even sing the “Row, Row, Row Your Boat” song!

WIND-DOWN WEDNESDAY

The Cloud Show
Take a moment to practice this mindfulness activity by watching the clouds go by. This will help bring you to the present moment and also help you to see that feelings come and go, just like clouds.

THEME THURSDAY

Sloth Yoga Poster
Try these sloth yoga poses, following the sequence listed on the poster to learn about the behavior of sloths. Try to hold each pose for a few breaths and imagine being a slow sloth.

FUN FRIDAY

Strike a Pose Game
Following the game instructions, clear some space and get out some music. This game is the yogi version of Freeze Dance, but instead, everyone strikes a pose when the music stops.

Figure Eight Breath

How to practice Figure Eight Breath

Take your pointer finger out in front of you. As you trace a figure 8 in the air, practice inhaling and exhaling deeply. Focus your eyes on your moving finger and feel your belly expand and contract with your deep belly breathing.

kidsyogastories.com

Row down the river

BOAT POSE

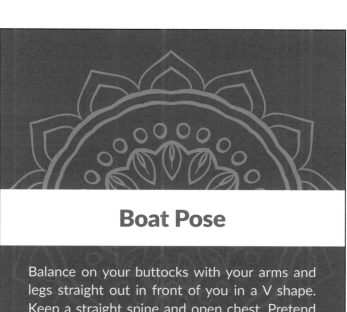

Boat Pose

Balance on your buttocks with your arms and legs straight out in front of you in a V shape. Keep a straight spine and open chest. Pretend to **row down the river**.

The Cloud Show

The Cloud Show

Watch clouds in the sky. Either lie on your back outdoors or pick a spot indoors to gaze at the clouds. Observe the clouds as they pass by and notice the various shapes. Talk about how your feelings drift by just like clouds do in the sky.

KIDS YOGA STORIES

kidsyogastories.com
© Kids Yoga Stories

SLOTH YOGA

I am a sloth moving slowly
up the trunk of a tree.

EAGLE POSE

I am a sloth slowly swimming
through the river.

LOCUST POSE

I am a sloth sleeping
on a branch.

EXTENDED CHILD'S POSE

I am a sloth hanging
upside-down from a branch.

HAPPY BABY POSE

I am a sloth tucking its head
in to sleep.

KNEES-TO-CHEST POSE

SLOTH YOGA

1. Pretend to be a sloth moving slowly up the trunk of a tree.

How to practice Eagle Pose: Wrap your left leg around your right. Bring your bent arms out in front of you, wrap your right arm around your left arm, and bend your knees slightly. Switch sides and repeat the steps. Pretend to be a sloth moving slowly up the trunk of a tree.

2. Pretend to be a sloth slowly swimming through the river.

How to practice Locust Pose: Lie on your tummy, lift your chest and shoulders, and look up. Slowly move your arms and legs, pretending to be a sloth swimming slowly across the river.

3. Pretend to be a sloth sleeping on a branch.

How to practice Extended Child's Pose: Come back to sit on your heels, slowly bring your forehead down to rest in front of your knees, place the palms of your hands flat out in front of you, and take a few deep breaths. Imagine being a sloth sleeping comfortably on a branch.

4. Pretend to be a sloth hanging upside-down from a branch.

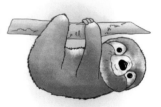

How to practice Happy Baby Pose: Lie on your back with your chin tucked in, hug your knees into your chest, then grab the outer parts of each foot—right foot in right hand and left foot in left hand. Pretend to be a sloth hanging upside-down from a branch.

5. Pretend to be a sloth tucking its head in to sleep.

How to practice Knees-to-Chest Pose: Lie on your back, bend your knees, and hug them close to your chest. Pretend to be a sloth tucking its head into its center to sleep.

KIDS YOGA STORIES

Strike a Pose

This game, adapted from Freeze Dance, is similar to Musical Chairs, but you don't need mats. Instead, encourage children to really let loose in their yogi dancing and be fully self-expressed.

What you need: music

HOW TO PLAY:

1. Space the players evenly around the room.

2. Once the music plays, the players all yogi dance around the room however they would like—creative movement is encouraged, as well as being safe.

3. When the music stops, everyone stops and strikes a yoga pose for a few moments without toppling over.

4. Music is played again, and play continues.

VARIATIONS:

- *Eliminate players who are moving when they are supposed to be striking a pose, like the traditional Freeze Dance game.*

- *Once the music stops, call out specific instructions for the pose choice, like "pick a balancing pose" or "pick an animal pose."*

- *To add color to the game, players could hold scarves or ribbons as they are dancing around.*

- *To extend the dancing idea, bring out a rope or long pole to play Yoga Limbo. Players take turns going under the pole in yoga poses, like walking Downward-Facing Dog Pose, jumping Squat Pose, or waddling in Reverse Table Top Pose.*

Classroom Yoga
IN 10 MINUTES A DAY
Week Eight

MINDFUL MONDAY

Creativity Meditation

Take a few minutes to read aloud the Creativity Meditation. Feel free to color the matching coloring page as you listen.

Twisty Tuesday

Pigeon Pose in a Chair

Try this chair yoga pose during a subject change throughout the day, when you return from recess and need to refocus, or if you just need a brain break.

WIND-DOWN WEDNESDAY

Garden Gnome Tree Pose Coloring Page

Get out your colored pencils or crayons to spend some relaxing time coloring in the garden gnomes. Put on some gentle music and talk about trees and forests. Try the pose with a partner.

THEME THURSDAY

Cowboy and Cowgirl Partner Yoga Poster

Try these country western yoga poses, following the sequence listed on the poster. These partner poses are meant to be practiced by two people who are working together to create the pose.

FUN FRIDAY

Pick a Pose Stick Game

Following the game instructions, get out some Popsicle sticks, a deck of yoga or breathing cards, and sticky notes to create your game. This game is great for one or more players.

Creativity

Close your eyes and imagine a wooden door with a rainbow painted on it.

You push open the door and step into a magical world of color.

Imagine walking up to an easel and picking up a paintbrush.

The colors flow across the canvas, and you paint the most beautiful painting you've ever seen.

Then you see a workbench with a hammer, nails, and brightly colored wooden blocks of all kinds of shapes and sizes.

Pick up the hammer and nail then build the most magnificent tree fort.

Inside your tree fort is a recording studio. Pick up a guitar and sit on a comfortable stool.

Imagine singing the coolest song you've ever heard.

Lastly, you head over to the dance studio, where there's a mirrored disco ball and lots of glitter.

You dance to the music like you've never danced before.

Your mind is bursting with excitement for this magical world you've discovered.

You're feeling immensely creative and inspired.

Take a few moments to absorb the creativity and imagination.

When you are ready, open your eyes.

kidsyogastories.com
© Kids Yoga Stories

Pigeon Pose

How to practice Pigeon Pose

Sit tall with your feet flat on the ground. Bend your right leg and place your right ankle on your left knee. Place your left hand on your right foot and your right hand on your right knee. Switch sides and repeat the steps.

KIDS YOGA STORIES

kidsyogastories.com
© Kids Yoga Stories

Tree Pose

COWBOY AND COWGIRL
PARTNER YOGA

Partner Warrior 1 Pose

Partner Warrior 2 Pose

Partner Warrior 3 Pose

Partner Horse Stance

Partner Standing
Locust Pose

KIDS YOGA STORIES

kidsyogastories.com

COWBOY AND COWGIRL PARTNER YOGA

This sequence includes poses meant to be practiced by two people who are working together to create the pose.

1. Partner Warrior 1 Pose

How to practice Warrior 1 Pose: Stand side by side, both facing forward. Plan your legs hip-width apart, feet facing forward, and straighten your arms alongside your body, standing tall. Step your outside foot back, angling your toes slightly outward. Bend your front knee, bring your arms straight up toward the sky, reaching for your partner's inside hand, and look up. Repeat on the other side.

2. Partner Warrior 2 Pose

How to practice Warrior 2 Pose: Stand next to each other, with your hips touching, and one partner facing forward while the other faces backward. Step your left foot back, placing the foot so that your toes are angled slightly outward. Take your arms up parallel to the ground, bend your front knee, and look forward. With your right hand, reach for your partner's left hand while wrapping your left hand back behind you and reaching for your partner's right hand. Take a few moments in this pose. Then switch sides and repeat the steps.

3. Partner Warrior 3 Pose

How to practice Warrior 3 Pose: Stand close next to each other, both facing forward. Stand on your inside leg. Extend the other outside leg behind you, flexing your foot. Bend your torso forward. Take your outside arm out to the side, and your right arm wraps around your partner's shoulders. Take a few moments in this pose, helping each other to balance. Switch sides and repeat the steps.

4. Partner Horse Stance

How to practice Horse Stance: Start with both partners facing the same direction, with one partner in front of the other. Stand with your legs apart, toes angled slightly outward. Bend your knees and stand firm as if you are riding a horse.

5. Partner Standing Locust Pose

How to practice Standing Locust Pose: Stand tall with your legs hip-width apart, toes pointing forward, and straighten your arms alongside your body. Shift so that you are standing back-to-back, a couple feet away from each other. Take your arms back and clasp hands with each other. Open your chest and squeeze your shoulders. Gently lean forward, arching into a baby backbend, with the support of your partner's hands behind you. Take a few moments in this position and then come to a neutral position.

Pick a Pose Stick

WHAT YOU NEED:	Popsicle sticks, deck of breathing cards, sticky notes
PLAYERS:	1 or more

HOW TO PLAY:

1. Write the numbers 1, 2, and 3 on large Popsicle sticks, one number on each stick.

2. Print out three yoga pose cards.

3. Write the numbers 1, 2, and 3 on sticky notes, one number on each note, and place one note on each of the yoga pose cards.

4. Pick out a numbered Popsicle stick.

5. Practice the pose with the corresponding number.

VARIATIONS:

- *Instead of pose cards, use partner poses, chair poses, or breathing exercise cards.*

- *Add more Popsicle sticks and pose cards as developmentally appropriate.*

- *Put the Popsicle sticks and cards in your Calm Down Corner for easy access.*

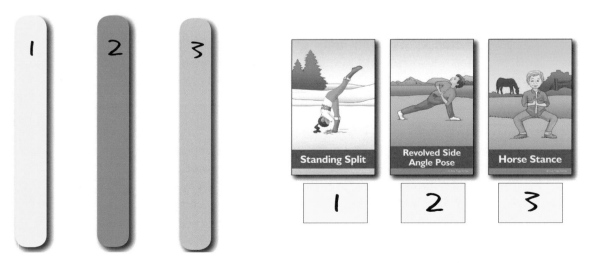

Classroom Yoga
IN 10 MINUTES A DAY
Week Nine

MINDFUL MONDAY

Positive Affirmation Cards (happy, hard-working, helpful)
Color the three affirmation cards with colored pencils or crayons, or feel free to use a different medium. Talk about the words and what they mean to you.

Twisty Tuesday

Eagle Pose
Perch like an eagle on a branch in Eagle Pose. Hold for a few moments and then try to bend your knees even further to take a deeper squat. Feel the stretch in your upper back, as well.

WIND-DOWN WEDNESDAY

Butterfly Coloring Page
Get out your colored pencils or crayons to spend some relaxing time coloring in the butterfly. Put on some gentle music and talk about butterflies or other animals you might find in the forest.

THEME THURSDAY

Be My Best Yoga Poster
Try these Be My Best yoga poses, following the sequence listed on the poster. Say the matching positive statement and hold each pose for a few breaths.

FUN FRIDAY

Yoga Pose Spinner
Following the game instructions, fill in your gameboard template with various poses. Spin the spinner and practice the pose that the paper clip lands on.

Perch like an eagle

EAGLE POSE

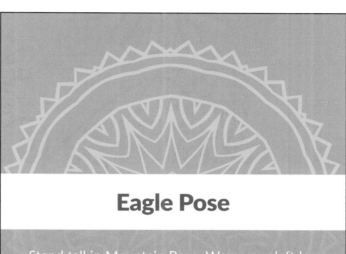

Eagle Pose

Stand tall in Mountain Pose. Wrap your left leg around your right. Bring your bent arms out in front of you, wrap your right arm around your left arm, and bend your knees slightly. Pretend to **perch like an eagle**. Switch sides and repeat the steps.

kidsyogastories.com
© Kids Yoga Stories

BE MY BEST YOGA

I am kind to all.
EASY POSE

I care about others.
SEATED SIDE BEND

I am a good listener.
CAT POSE

I am generous.
COW POSE

I am mindful.
CHILD'S POSE

BE MY BEST YOGA

This sequence includes mantras, which you may say aloud to yourself or repeat in your mind.
Try to link the mantra to your breath once you are in the pose.

1. I am kind to all.

How to practice Easy Pose: Sit cross-legged and rest your palms on your knees. Close your eyes, if you are comfortable doing so. Take a few deep breaths and relax your body. "I am kind to all."

2. I care about others.

How to practice Seated Side Bend: Come to sitting comfortably cross-legged. Place your right hand flat on the ground straight out to the side. Then reach your left hand over your head, tilting your upper body to the right. Keep your buttocks on the ground. Feel the gentle stretch in your left side. Come back to center and repeat on the other side. "I care about others."

3. I am a good listener.

How to practice Cat Pose: On all fours, round your back and tuck your chin into your chest. "I am a good listener."

4. I am generous.

How to practice Cow Pose: On all fours, look up, arch your back, and open your chest. "I am generous."

5. I am mindful.

How to practice Child's Pose: Sit on your heels, slowly bring your forehead down to rest on the floor in front of your knees, rest your arms down alongside your body, and take a few deep breaths. "I am mindful."

KIDS
YOGA
STORIES

kidsyogastories.com
© Kids Yoga Stories

Yoga Pose Spinner

What you need: Yoga Pose Spinner gameboard, pencil, and paper clip

HOW TO PLAY:

1. Fill in your Yoga Pose Spinner gameboard with various poses.

2. You could also add a number or math problem to signal how long to hold the pose.

3. Place the tip of the pencil through the end of the paper clip and then press it to the middle of the spinner where the lines intersect.

4. Hold the pencil steady and spin the paper clip around the spinner.

5. Spin the spinner then practice the pose that the paper clip lands on.

6. Play continues taking turns for each player.

SAMPLE GAME

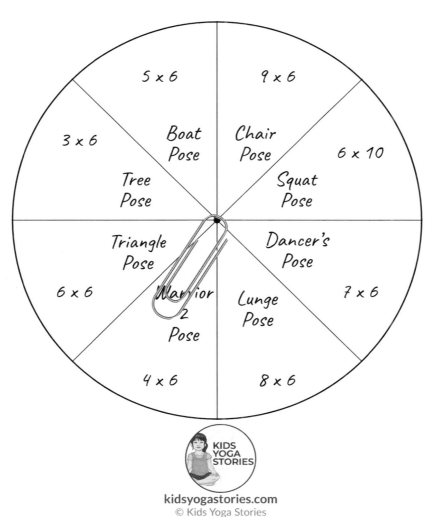

Yoga Pose Spinner

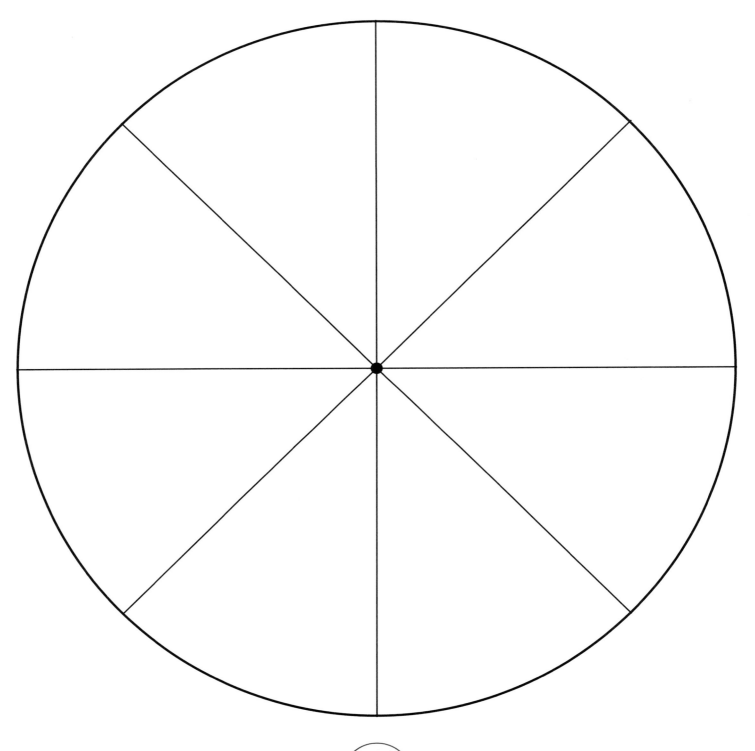

Classroom Yoga
IN 10 MINUTES A DAY
Week Ten

MINDFUL MONDAY

Candle Breath

Take a moment to practice Candle Breath throughout the day. Model it for your children and talk about the benefits of taking a moment to take a deep breath.

Twisty Tuesday

Wide-Legged Forward Bend in a Chair

Try this chair yoga pose during a subject change throughout the day, when you return from recess and need to refocus, or if you just need a brain break.

WIND-DOWN WEDNESDAY

Eagle Pose Coloring Page

Get out your colored pencils or crayons to spend some relaxing time coloring in the eagle pose page. Put on some gentle music and maybe talk about what you love to do in the winter.

THEME THURSDAY

Winter Activities Yoga Poster

Try these winter activities yoga poses, following the sequence listed on the poster. Pretend to be snowshoeing, skating, and sledding.

FUN FRIDAY

What Time Is It, Yogi?

Following the game instructions, get out dice, deck of yoga cards, and a teaching clock to create your game board. Play in partners or a small group to practice addition and telling time to the hour.

Candle Breath

How to practice Candle Breath

Clasp your fingers together and extended your pointer fingers up like a steeple. Pretending to be holding a candle, bring your steepled hands in front of your mouth. Take a deep breath in through your nose then pretend to blow out your candle. Close your eyes, if that's comfortable. Repeat a few times.

kidsyogastories.com

Wide-Legged Forward Bend

How to practice Wide-Legged Forward Bend

Stand tall with your legs hip-width apart in front of your chair, feet facing forward, and straighten your arms alongside your body. Then, step your feet out wide, bend your upper body, and take your hands to the back of the chair. Bend your arms and rest your forehead on the front of your chair. Feel the gentle stretch in your legs.

KIDS YOGA STORIES

kidsyogastories.com

kidsyogastories.com
© Kids Yoga Stories

WINTER ACTIVITIES

Pretend to be snowshoeing.
MOUNTAIN POSE VARIATION

Pretend to be skating.
WARRIOR 3 POSE

Pretend to be skiing.
CHAIR POSE

Pretend to be sledding.
STAFF POSE

Pretend to be making snow angels.
RESTING POSE

WINTER ACTIVITIES

1. Pretend to be snowshoeing.

How to practice Mountain Pose variation: Stand tall with legs hip-width apart and feet facing forward. Gently swing your bent arms back and forth while walking on the spot as if you are snowshoeing.

2. Pretend to be skating.

How to practice Warrior 3 Pose: Stand on one leg. Extend the other leg behind you. Bend your torso forward and take your arms out behind you to pretend you are gliding on the ice like a figure skater.

3. Pretend to be skiing.

How to practice Chair Pose: Stand tall in Mountain Pose with your feet hip-width apart, bend your knees, and pretend to ski down the slopes like a skier.

4. Pretend to be sledding.

How to practice Staff Pose: Sit with a tall spine and your legs straight out in front of you. Take your hands down beside you and pretend to hold on to the sled as you fly down a snowy hill.

5. Pretend to be making snow angels.

How to practice Resting Pose: Lie on your back with your arms and legs stretched out like a star. Move your arms and legs in unison as if you are making a snow angel. Breathe and rest.

KIDS
YOGA
STORIES

kidsyogastories.com
© Kids Yoga Stories

82

What Time Is It, Yogi?

What you need:	dice, deck of yoga cards, teaching clock (optional)
Math skills:	telling time to the hour, addition
Players:	2 or more

HOW TO PLAY:

1. Get out a teaching clock or draw your own clock with the hour hand drawn in.

2. Place twelve yoga cards around the clock in each of the hour slots.

3. Player One rolls the dice, adds the two numbers together, then practices the yoga pose found at that corresponding o'clock.

   For example: Player One rolls 2 and 5. Since 2 + 5 = 7, the player practices the pose on the card at the seven o'clock mark.

4. Next, Player Two rolls the two dice and practices that corresponding pose.

5. Play continues until they have practiced all the poses around the clock.

6. The players can roll one die to try to get the number 1, to be able to practice the yoga pose at one o'clock.

VARIATIONS:

- *Change the yoga pose cards once they have all been practiced and play again.*

- *Include a minute hand, either drawn or placed, at quarter past, half past, or quarter to the hour.*

KIDS
YOGA
STORIES

kidsyogastories.com
© Kids Yoga Stories

Classroom Yoga
IN 10 MINUTES A DAY
Week Eleven

MINDFUL MONDAY

Happiness Meditation

Take a few minutes to read aloud the Happiness Meditation. Feel free to color the matching coloring page as you listen.

Twisty Tuesday

Warrior 2 Pose

Pretend to surf the waves like a surfer in Warrior 2 Pose. Hold for a few moments and then switch sides and repeat the steps. Imagine the wind going through your hair.

WIND-DOWN WEDNESDAY

Rainstorm Hands

Take a moment to practice this mindfulness activity by creating a rainstorm in your hands. This will help bring you to the present moment and calm your mind.

THEME THURSDAY

Core Yoga Poster

Try these yoga poses, following the sequence listed on the poster to build your core strength. Try to hold each pose for as long as you can – even up to a minute long.

FUN FRIDAY

I'm Going to Yoga Class Game

Following the game instructions, create a long sequence of yoga poses by having each player add a new pose at their turn. See how many poses you can remember in a row!

Happiness

Close your eyes and take a moment to be still.

Pretend you're in a meadow covered with scented wildflowers.

You feel the warm breeze on your face. The chirp of birds fills the spring air.

Now imagine running barefoot across the soft ground.

You skip and twirl, chasing a bright-blue butterfly.

You lie on the sweet-smelling grass and look up at the wispy clouds.

Your mind is full of happy thoughts. You are simply living in the moment.

Your heart is full. You feel endlessly happy and free.

When you are ready, open your eyes.

Surf the waves

WARRIOR 2 POSE

Warrior 2 Pose

Start in a standing position. Step one foot back, bend your front knee, and open your hips to the side. Then reach both arms up, parallel to your legs, and look over your front fingertips. Make sure your front knee is bent forward so that your knee is over your ankle. Pretend to **surf the waves**. Switch sides and repeat the steps.

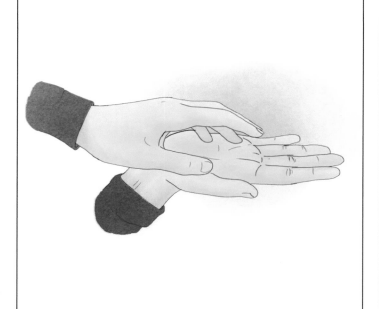

Rainstorm Hands

Rainstorm Hands

Play a "rainstorm" in your hand. Start by touching the fingers of your right hand on your left palm. Then tap your fingers like a sprinkle of rain. Then pat all of your fingers together into your palm, progressing to a clap. End with cupping your hands. Finish by reversing the rainstorm to a light pitter-patter before bringing your hands together.

CORE YOGA

 **Crow Pose**

 **Plank Pose**

 **Dolphin Pose**

 **Scale Pose**

 **Boat Pose**

CORE YOGA

1. Crow Pose

How to practice Crow Pose: From a squat position, place your palms flat on the ground out in front of you. Place your knees gently on the back of your upper arms. Tilt forward to lift your toes off the ground and balance on your bent arms, looking forward.

2. Plank Pose

How to practice Plank Pose: Step back to balance on your palms and on your bent toes in a plank position. Keep your arms straight and your back long and flat.

3. Dolphin Pose

How to practice Dolphin Pose: On your hands and knees, bend your elbows and rest your forearms on the ground, keeping your palms flat on the ground. Lift your knees to straighten your legs and then look forward.

4. Scale Pose

How to practice Scale Pose: Come to sitting comfortably cross-legged or in Lotus Pose. Place your palms flat on the ground outside your thighs. Lean forward slightly, press into your hands, and lift your buttocks and legs off the ground. Hold for a few breaths then slowly lower to the ground.

5. Boat Pose

How to practice Boat Pose: Balance on your buttocks with your arms and legs straight out in front of you in a V shape. Keep a straight spine and open chest.

I'm Going to Yoga Class

This game, adapted from "I'm Going on a Picnic" or "I'm Going to Grandmother's House," encourages children to focus and practice their listening skills. They also learn how to build yoga sequences, linking several poses together.

What you need: yoga pose cards (optional)

HOW TO PLAY:

1. The players stand in a circle.

2. The first player says, "I'm going to yoga class, and I'm practicing [specific pose]." The player then demonstrates that pose to the group.

3. The next player repeats what the first player did then adds their own pose.

4. The play continues, building the yoga sequence, until a player can't remember the order. Then that player is excused from the game.

5. Play continues until all the players can't remember the order.

6. The goal of the game is to build the longest sequence possible.

VARIATIONS:

*   *The players could pick a pose from a card deck for their turn rather than making up their own.*

*   *Change the wording to suit your theme or group. For example, "I love yoga, and my favorite pose is…"*

*   *The players could all help each other if someone forgets the sequence, creating a more cooperative game.*

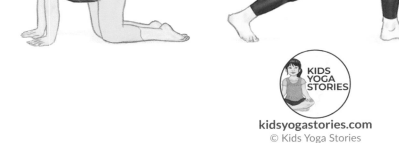

KIDS
YOGA
STORIES

Classroom Yoga
IN 10 MINUTES A DAY
Week Twelve

MINDFUL MONDAY

Positive Affirmation Cards (creative, curious, cooperative)
Color the three affirmation cards with colored pencils or crayons, or feel free to use a different medium. Talk about the words and what they mean to you.

Twisty Tuesday

Downward-Facing Dog Pose in a Chair
Try this chair yoga pose during a subject change throughout the day, when you return from recess and need to refocus, or if you just need a brain break.

WIND-DOWN WEDNESDAY

Garden Gnome Seated Cat Pose Coloring Page
Get out your colored pencils or crayons to spend some relaxing time coloring in the garden gnomes. Put on some gentle music and chat about your day. Try the pose with a partner.

THEME THURSDAY

Superhero Partner Yoga Poster
Try these superhero yoga poses, following the sequence listed on the poster. These partner poses are meant to be practiced by two people who are working together to create the pose.

FUN FRIDAY

Build the Poses Game
Following the game instructions, get out a deck of yoga pose cards to play a game of building on poses to create a sequence. Have fun practicing your yoga sequence.

I am creative.

© Kids Yoga Stories

I am curious.

© Kids Yoga Stories

I am cooperative.

© Kids Yoga Stories

94

Downward-Facing Dog Pose

How to practice Downward-Facing Dog Pose

Come to standing just in front of your chair, facing the chair. Place your hands flat on the front of the chair and slowly step back so that your arms are stretched out straight in front of you. Straighten your spine, ensure your legs are hip-width apart, and look down between your legs.

Seated Cat Pose

KIDS
YOGA
STORIES

kidsyogastories.com
© Kids Yoga Stories

SUPERHERO PARTNER YOGA

This sequence includes poses meant to be practiced by two people who are working together to create the pose. The mantras can be spoken aloud together or repeated in your mind.

We listen to each other.
EXTENDED MOUNTAIN POSE

We are powerful.
REVERSE WARRIOR POSE

We are a team.
TRIANGLE POSE

We are problem solvers.
BACK-TO-BACK CHAIR POSE

We are thoughtful.
FORWARD BEND

SUPERHERO PARTNER YOGA

This sequence includes poses meant to be practiced by two people who are working together to create the pose. The mantras can be spoken aloud together or repeated in your mind.

1. We listen to each other.

How to practice Extended Mountain Pose: Stand tall in Mountain Pose with your legs hip-width apart, facing each other, about two arms' lengths away from each other. Take your arms straight up to the sky and touch your palms together. In sync with your partner, lean your torso forward and press your palms against your partner's palms. Be in communication (through words or body language) to help balance each other. Come out of the pose when you're both ready. "We listen to each other."

2. We are powerful.

How to practice Reverse Warrior Pose: Come to a standing position facing away from each other about two legs' lengths away from each other. Then turn toward each other, step your inside foot back, angling your toes slightly outward. Your back feet should be almost touching together. Then raise your arms parallel to the floor. Bend your front knee and look forward. Flip your outside palm up to the sky, tilt your torso backward, and rest your left hand on your left thigh. Look up at your extended hand, reach for your partner's hand overhead, open your chest, and keep your spine long and straight. Come back to center and repeat on the other side. "We are powerful."

3. We are a team.

How to practice Triangle Pose: Stand together, back-to-back. Step the outside foot back, angling the foot slightly outward. Take your arms up parallel to the floor, bend at the waist, and tilt your upper body forward. Reach your front inside hand to gently rest on your shin and stretch your other arm straight up, reaching for your partner's hand at the top. Switch sides and repeat the steps. "We are a team."

4. We are problem solvers.

How to practice Back-to-Back Chair Pose: Facing each other, stand tall in Mountain Pose with your feet hip-width apart. Reach out and grab your partner's hands in front of you. Bend your knees and keep a straight spine. Sit down into an imaginary chair and lean back, relying on the support of your partner's grasp. Sit as deeply as feels comfortable for both partners. Come out of the pose at the same time. "We are problem solvers."

5. We are thoughtful.

How to practice Forward Bend: Stand tall with legs hip-width apart, feet facing forward, and straighten your arms alongside your body. Shift so that you're facing each other about two legs' lengths away from each other. Bend your upper body and reach your arms to rest on your partner's shoulders. Your heads should almost be touching, and your arms should be fully supported by your partner. Take a few deep breaths and relax into the pose, feeling the stretch in your lower back. "We are thoughtful."

kidsyogastories.com
© Kids Yoga Stories

Build the Poses

WHAT YOU NEED:	pose cards
PLAYERS:	2 or more

HOW TO PLAY:

1. The first person does a pose (or you can pick a pose from a Yoga Pose Card Deck).

2. The second person does that first pose then adds another pose to the sequence.

3. The first (or next) person then does the first two poses and adds another pose.

4. Play continues as long as you like, building up the yoga sequence.

SAMPLE OF THE GAME:

Player 1: Tree Pose.

Player 2: Tree Pose. Dancer's Pose.

Player 1: Tree Pose. Dancer's Pose. Warrior 3 Pose.

Player 2: Tree Pose. Dancer's Pose. Warrior 3 Pose. Warrior 2 Pose.

Player 1: Tree Pose. Dancer's Pose. Warrior 3 Pose. Warrior 2 Pose. Squat Pose.

Classroom Yoga
IN 10 MINUTES A DAY
Week Thirteen

MINDFUL MONDAY

Take 5 Breath

Take a moment to practice Take 5 Breath throughout the day. Model it for your children and talk about the benefits of taking a moment to take a deep breath.

Twisty Tuesday

Dancer's Pose

Express yourself like a dancer in Dancer's Pose. Hold for a few moments and then switch sides and repeat the steps. See how long you can balance on one leg.

WIND-DOWN WEDNESDAY

Peacock Coloring Page

Get out your colored pencils or crayons to spend some relaxing time coloring in the peacock. Put on some gentle music and talk about peacocks or other exotic and interesting animals.

THEME THURSDAY

Empathy Partner Yoga Poster

Try these empathy yoga poses, following the sequence listed on the poster. Say the matching positive statement as you both work together to create the partner pose.

FUN FRIDAY

Spell Your Pose Flow Game

Following the game instructions, fill in your gameboard template with a different pose for each letter of the alphabet. Choose a word and then perform the pose matching each letter of the word.

Take 5 Breath

How to practice Take 5 Breath

Take your right hand and spread your fingers like a star. Place your left pointer finger at the base of your right pinky finger. As you take a deep inhale, slide your pointer finger up your pinky finger. Pause briefly at the top of the finger. Then exhale fully while tracing the inside of your pinky finger. Repeat the inhale up your ring finger and exhale down your ring finger. Continue tracing your fingers and matching to your breath until you come to the outside of your thumb after five deep inhales and exhales. You can also trace your left hand if that's more comfortable.

kidsyogastories.com
© Kids Yoga Stories

Express yourself like a dancer

DANCER'S POSE

Dancer's Pose

Stand tall in Mountain Pose. Then stand on your right leg, reach your left leg out behind you, and place the outside of your left foot into your left hand. Bend your torso forward, with your right arm out in front for balance, and arch your leg up behind you. Pretend to **express yourself like a dancer**. Switch sides and repeat the steps.

kidsyogastories.com
© Kids Yoga Stories

EMPATHY YOGA

We listen to each other.
PARTNER EXTENDED MOUNTAIN POSE

We connect and understand.
PARTNER BOAT POSE

We are compassionate.
SEESAW

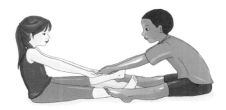

We are kind to each other.
LIZARD ON A ROCK

We feel empathy.
PARTNER EASY POSE

KIDS
YOGA
STORIES

kidsyogastories.com

EMPATHY YOGA

This sequence includes poses meant to be practiced by two people who are working together to create the pose.

1. We listen to each other.

How to practice Partner Extended Mountain Pose: Stand tall in Mountain Pose with your legs hip-width apart, facing each other, about two arms' lengths away from each other. Take your arms straight up to the sky and touch your palms together. In sync with your partner, lean your torso forward and press your palms against your partner's palms. Be in communication (through words or body language) to help balance each other. Come out of the pose when you're both ready.

2. We connect and understand.

How to practice Partner Boat Pose: Sit facing each other with your bent legs out in front of you. Grab hands and inch your feet together until they are touching. Press into each other's feet and lift your legs. Balance on your buttocks and try to straighten your legs into a V position. Hold the pose for a few moments before slowly coming down.

3. We are compassionate.

How to practice Seesaw: Sit in an L position facing each other. You could either press your flexed feet together, or one person could bring their feet inside their partner's legs. Reach forward and grab each other's hands. To begin the seesaw, one partner leans back, bringing the other partner forward. Each partner takes a turn leaning back then bending forward to create the seesaw. Try this back-and-forth movement a few times.

4. We are kind to each other.

How to practice Lizard on a Rock: The first partner comes to an all-fours position. Then shift back to place your buttocks on your heels. Slowly bring your forehead down to rest in between your knees, rest your arms down alongside your body, and take a few deep breaths in Child's Pose. Once you are in a comfortable resting position, pretending to be a rock, the second partner can slowly place her buttocks on your lower back and begin to recline so that her back is lying on your spine and her head rests on your upper back. Encourage the second partner to open up and relax completely. To come out of the pose, gently lift your torso while helping your partner to slowly stand up.

5. We feel empathy.

How to practice Partner Easy Pose: Come to sitting in a comfortable cross-legged position back-to-back with your partner. Take a few deep breaths together. Close your eyes and feel the rise and fall of your partner's breath. Take the opportunity to tune in to how your partner might be feeling at this moment.

KIDS YOGA STORIES

kidsyogastories.com
© Kids Yoga Stories

Spell Your Pose Flow

What you need: Spell Your Pose Flow gameboard

HOW TO PLAY:

1. Get out your Spell Your Pose gameboard and write a pose beside each letter of the alphabet.

2. Take turns choosing a word and spelling it by performing the pose matching each letter of the word.

3. Continue play for as long as you like.

SAMPLE GAME

Spell a word and hold each pose for ten counts!

A . Boat Pose	**N** . Cobbler's Pose
B . Plank Pose	**O** . Downward Dog Pose
C . Triangle Pose	**P** . Eagle Pose
D . Staff Pose	**Q** . Squat Pose
E . Lunge Pose	**R** . Hero Pose
F . Tree Pose	**S** . Extended Side Angle
G . Flower Pose	**T** . Standing Forward Bend
H . Child's Pose	**U** . Crescent Moon Pose
I . Chair Pose	**V** . Dolphin Pose
J . Warrior 2 Pose	**W** . Extended Cat Pose
K . Dancer's Pose	**X** . Seated Twist
L . Warrior 3 Pose	**Y** . Pigeon Pose
M . Cat-Cow Flow	**Z** . Wide-Legged Forward Bend

Spell Your Pose Flow

Spell a word and hold each pose for ten counts!

A •	N •
B •	O •
C •	P •
D •	Q •
E •	R •
F •	S •
G •	T •
H •	U •
I •	V •
J •	W •
K •	X •
L •	Y •
M •	Z •

KIDS
YOGA
STORIES

kidsyogastories.com
© Kids Yoga Stories

Classroom Yoga
IN 10 MINUTES A DAY
Week Fourteen

MINDFUL MONDAY

Power Breath

Take a moment to practice Power Breath throughout the day. Model it for your children and talk about the benefits of taking a moment to take a powerful breath to feel energized.

Twisty Tuesday

Side Bend in a Chair

Try this chair yoga pose during a subject change throughout the day, when you return from recess and need to refocus, or if you just need a brain break.

WIND-DOWN WEDNESDAY

Cobbler's Pose Coloring Page

Get out your colored pencils or crayons to spend some relaxing time coloring in the cobbler's pose page. Put on some gentle music and maybe talk about what active things you like to do.

THEME THURSDAY

Energizing Yoga Poster

Try these yoga poses, following the sequence listed on the poster to build heat in your body. Try to hold each pose for as long as you can – even up to a minute long.

FUN FRIDAY

Odd or Even Poses Game

Following the game instructions, get out dice, deck of yoga cards, and deck of breathing cards to create the game. Play in partners or a small group to practice addition or odds and evens.

Power Breath

How to practice Power Breath

Clench your hands into fists above your head then exhale vigorously through your mouth, saying, "Ha!" At the same time, bring your fists quickly to your chest while tucking your elbows against your body. Think of pulling the power of the sun into your body through your chest. Repeat this breathing technique a few times to bring warmth to your body. You can also try it with one arm at a time.

kidsyogastories.com
© Kids Yoga Stories

Side Bend

How to practice Side Bend

Sit tall on your chair with your feet flat on the ground and your palms on your knees. Then take your left arm straight up to the sky. Tilt your upper body to the right and place your right hand on the chair. Open your chest, look up, and feel the gentle stretch on the left side of your body. Come back to center. Switch sides and repeat the sides.

KIDS
YOGA
STORIES

kidsyogastories.com
© Kids Yoga Stories

ENERGIZING YOGA

 **Warrior 1 Pose**

 **Chair Pose**

 **Dolphin Plank Pose**

 **Lizard Pose**

 **Crow Pose**

ENERGIZING YOGA

1. Warrior 1 Pose

How to practice Warrior 1 Pose: Step one foot back, angling your toes slightly outward, and bend your front knee. Reach both arms up overhead. Switch sides and repeat the steps.

2. Chair Pose

How to practice Chair Pose: Stand tall in Mountain Pose with your feet hip-width apart, bend your knees, and keep a straight spine. Hold your hands out in front of you.

3. Dolphin Plank Pose

How to practice Dolphin Plank Pose: Step back to a plank position on your toes. Bend your arms and come down to rest on your elbows with your forearms parallel out in front of you and palms flat on the ground. Imagine a straight line from your toes to your head. Hold this position for a couple of breaths and then rest.

4. Lizard Pose

How to practice Lizard Pose: From Downward-Facing Dog Pose, shift forward to bring your shoulders over your wrists. Gently place your right foot on the outside of your right hand, with your right foot facing forward. Stay in this deep lunge for a moment. If you're able, drop your elbows to the ground for a deeper stretch. Reverse the steps to come out of the pose. Switch sides and repeat the steps.

5. Crow Pose

How to practice Crow Pose: From a squat position, place your palms flat on the ground out in front of you. Place your knees gently on the back of your upper arms. Tilt forward to lift your toes off the ground and balance on your bent arms, looking forward.

KIDS YOGA STORIES

kidsyogastories.com
© Kids Yoga Stories

Odd or Even Poses

WHAT YOU NEED:	dice, deck of yoga cards (only the pose cards), deck of breathing cards
MATH SKILLS:	addition, even and odd
PLAYERS:	2 or more

HOW TO PLAY:

1. Each player rolls a die.

2. The two players add the two numbers they have rolled.

3. If the number is even, strike a pose by selecting a pose card. If the number is odd, select a breathing card and try that breathing technique. Practice the pose and breathe for five counts.

4. Play continues for a certain amount of time or until the deck is finished.

VARIATIONS:

- *Play with three players and add all three numbers together.*

- *Instead of a breathing card, use partner poses.*

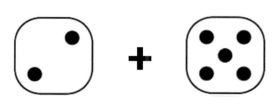

Classroom Yoga
IN 10 MINUTES A DAY
Week Fifteen

MINDFUL MONDAY

Positive Affirmation Cards (relaxed, respectful, responsible)
Color the three affirmation cards with colored pencils or crayons, or feel free to use a different medium. Talk about the words and what they mean to you.

Twisty Tuesday

Extended Side Angle Pose
Pretend to be sailing like a windsurfer in Extended Side Angle Pose. Hold for a few moments and then switch legs and repeat the steps. Imagine the smell and sounds of the ocean.

WIND-DOWN WEDNESDAY

The Great Outdoors
Take a moment to practice this mindfulness activity by going outside in nature to awaken your senses. This will help bring you to the present moment and calm your mind.

THEME THURSDAY

Yoga Inversions Poster
Try these yoga poses, following the sequence listed on the poster to turn your world upside-down and help you change perspective. Take a few deep breaths in the pose.

FUN FRIDAY

Follow the Yogi Game
This ice-breaker game has been adapted from the common kids game Follow the Leader and is a great game to help students learn each other's names.

I am
relaxed.

© Kids Yoga Stories

I am
respectful.

© Kids Yoga Stories

I am
responsible.

© Kids Yoga Stories

Sail like a windsurfer

EXTENDED SIDE ANGLE POSE

Extended Side Angle Pose

Stand tall in Mountain Pose. Step one foot back, slightly angling it outward. Keep your torso straight and bend your front leg. Tilt your upper body forward, rest your front elbow on your thigh (or take your hand to the floor). Reach your other arm straight up to the sky and look up toward your hand. Pretend to **sail like a windsurfer**. Repeat on the other side.

The Great Outdoors

The Great Outdoors

Go outside in nature to awaken your senses. What do you smell? What sounds do you hear? What could you hold in your hand? What do you see?

KIDS
YOGA
STORIES

kidsyogastories.com
© Kids Yoga Stories

YOGA INVERSIONS

 Forward Bend
Chest Stretch

 Wide-Legged
Forward Bend

 Three-Legged Dog Pose

 Puppy Pose

 Thread the Needle Pose

KIDS
YOGA
STORIES

YOGA INVERSIONS

1. Forward Bend Chest Stretch

How to practice Forward Bend Chest Stretch: Come to a standing position with your feet hip-width apart. Clasp your hands together behind your back (or grab a strap if your shoulders are tight). Slowly bend your torso forward and drop your head toward the ground. Allow your clasped hands to stretch up behind you.

2. Wide-Legged Forward Bend

How to practice Wide-Legged Forward Bend: Stand tall with legs hip-width apart, feet facing forward, and straighten your arms alongside your body. Step your feet out wide, bend your upper body, and reach your palms to the ground.

3. Three-Legged Dog Pose

How to practice Three-Legged Dog Pose: From Downward-Facing Dog Pose (upside-down V shape), gently lift one leg at a time with a flexed foot. Ensure you keep your arms and spine straight when you lift a leg.

4. Puppy Pose

How to practice Puppy Pose: From all fours, slide your hands out in front of you while lowering your chest toward the ground. Keep your arms straight and raise your elbows off the ground. Rest your forehead between your extended arms, letting your spine curve naturally.

5. Thread the Needle Pose

How to practice Thread the Needle Pose: Come to an all-fours position in Table Top Pose. On an inhale, take your right hand straight up to the sky, look up, and feel the twist. On an exhale, take your right hand (palm up) and thread it straight underneath your left arm. Place your right shoulder and right cheek on the mat. Your hips and left elbow are still raised as you relax into the ground, gazing out to the left. Gently come out of the pose and then repeat on the other side.

Follow the Yogi

Follow the Leader (also known as Indian Chief) is a common ice-breaker game, and Follow the Yogi is perfect for the first day of class, to help students learn each other's names.

What you need: yoga pose cards (optional)

HOW TO PLAY:

1. Choose one player to be the "guru" (or "detective").

2. Send this player somewhere they can't see the rest of the players (or have them cover their eyes).

3. The rest of the players stand in a circle and (quietly) choose a "yogi" to be the secret leader. This secret leader will practice a series of poses for the players to follow without looking directly at the leader. (They might need to try it once or twice before bringing the guru back.)

4. Bring the guru back into the room.

5. The group will follow the secret yogi, performing the sequence, while the guru watches closely, trying to determine who the secret yogi leader is.

6. The game ends once the guru has correctly identified the yogi.

7. The yogi then becomes the guru and goes outside while the next Yogi is chosen.

8. Play continues as long as you would like.

VARIATIONS:

- *Go over a number of poses before the game starts so that players are familiar with a bunch of poses.*

- *Give the guru a certain number of guesses before revealing the yogi's identity.*

Classroom Yoga
IN 10 MINUTES A DAY
Week Sixteen

MINDFUL MONDAY

Hope Meditation

Take a few minutes to read aloud the Hope Meditation. Feel free to color the matching coloring page as you listen.

Twisty Tuesday

Triangle Forward Bend in a Chair

Try this chair yoga pose during a subject change throughout the day, when you return from recess and need to refocus, or if you just need a brain break.

WIND-DOWN WEDNESDAY

Garden Gnome Gate Pose Coloring Page

Get out your colored pencils or crayons to spend some relaxing time coloring in the garden gnomes. Put on some gentle music and talk about what your summer plans. Try the pose with a partner.

THEME THURSDAY

Garden Gnome Partner Yoga Poster

Try these yoga poses, following the sequence listed on the poster to build your core strength. Try to hold each pose for as long as you can – even up to a minute long.

FUN FRIDAY

Yoga Board Game

Following the DIY instructions, create your own yoga gameboard using the template provided. Get out your dice and game pieces, and have fun playing the game!

125

Hope

Come to sitting silently. Take a few deep breaths. Close your eyes.

Imagine you are walking down a gravel path in the countryside.

You see tall trees and colorful flowers lining the pathway.

Rays of sunshine peek through the trees. Birds are chirping. There's a light breeze.

You smile as you take in a full breath to smell the fresh air.

You look ahead, and the path runs as far as your eyes can see.

With each step you take, you start to feel more confident and positive.

The long path ahead makes it feel like life has given you lots of options.

You have so much ahead of you. Your future is bright.

Take a moment to feel positive about the future.

When you are ready, open your eyes.

Triangle Forward Bend

How to practice Triangle Forward Bend

Stand tall with legs hip-width apart in front of your chair, feet facing forward, and straighten your arms alongside your body. Take your right foot back, keeping your ankle bent at a thirty-degree angle. Place your hands on the front of the chair, ensuring that your back is flat and that you are looking straight ahead. Then slowly bend forward as if your hips are a hinge, keeping a flat back and a long neck. Check that your spine is straight. Repeat on the other side.

KIDS YOGA STORIES

kidsyogastories.com
© Kids Yoga Stories

Gate Pose

GARDEN GNOME PARTNER YOGA

This sequence includes poses meant to be practiced by
two people who are working together to create the pose.

Partner Tree Pose

Partner Dancer's Pose

Partner Chair Pose

Partner Gate Pose

Partner Flower Pose

KIDS
YOGA
STORIES

kidsyogastories.com

GARDEN GNOME PARTNER YOGA

This sequence includes poses meant to be practiced by two people who are working together to create the pose.

1. Partner Tree Pose

How to practice Tree Pose: Stand next to each other, either holding hands or with your arms around each other's waist. Stand tall with your shoulders back, head up, spine straight, and legs firmly planted into the ground. Then shift to stand on your inner leg—you'll be creating a mirror image with your partner. Bend your other leg, place the sole of your foot on your inner thigh or calf (just not on your knee), and help each other to balance. If you feel steady, take your outer arm and reach up to the sky. You could also sway together like trees in the wind. Switch sides and repeat the steps.

2. Partner Dancer's Pose

How to practice Dancer's Pose: Stand tall in Mountain Pose, facing each other, about two arms' lengths away from each other. Stand on your right leg, reach your left leg out behind you, and place the outside of your left foot into your left hand. Bend your torso forward, take your partner's hand for balance, and arch your leg up behind you as if you are a dancer. Hold the pose for a few breaths and then signal each other to come out of the pose at the same time. Switch sides and repeat the steps.

3. Partner Chair Pose

How to practice Chair Pose: Stand tall in Mountain Pose with your feet hip-width apart while facing each other. Reach out and grab your partner's hands in front of you. bend your knees and keep a straight spine. Sit down into an imaginary chair and lean back, relying on the support of your partner's grasp. Sit as deeply as feels comfortable for both partners. Come out of the pose at the same time.

4. Partner Gate Pose

How to practice Gate Pose: Come to a kneeling position beside your partner, both facing forward, about two legs' lengths away from each other. Take your inside leg straight out to the middle of you both. Inhale and bring your outside arm up, parallel to the ground. Exhale and tilt inward, extending your outside arm straight up grabbing your partner's hand overhead and placing your inside hand on the shin of your extended leg. Take a few deep breaths, making sure your hips and shoulders are facing forward, and that your chest is open. Come out of the pose at the same time.

5. Partner Flower Pose

How to practice Flower Pose: Come to sit on your buttocks with a tall spine and bent legs in front of you. Shift so that you are facing each other about two legs' lengths away from each together. Lift your bent legs and balance on your sitting bones. Grab each other's hands (between your legs) while touching your feet together and raising them as high as is comfortable. Open your chest and ensure that your spine is straight. Use your connected hands and feet to steady your balance, find a still position in Flower Pose, and take a few deep breaths. Come out of the pose at the same time.

Yoga Board Game

What you need: Yoga Board Game gameboard, 1 die, and game pieces (for example, little figurines or coins)

HOW TO PLAY:

1. Get out the Yoga Board Game template or draw your own gameboard on large paper.

2. Add your own yoga poses or breathing techniques to the squares.

3. Add other options such as moving forward, going back, or missing a turn.

4. Add other learning opportunities like math problems or science questions.

5. Players put their game pieces on the Start square.

6. Players take turns rolling one die and moving their game piece around the board and doing the activity in the squares.

7. The winner is the first player to cross the finish line.

SAMPLE GAME

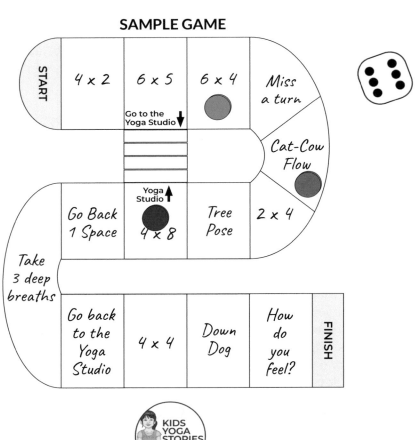

kidsyogastories.com
© Kids Yoga Stories

Yoga Board Game

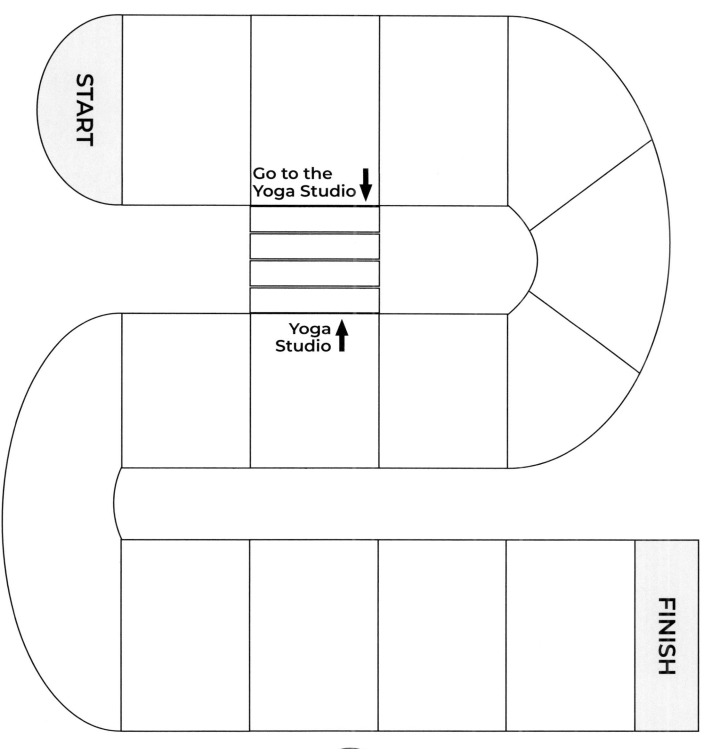

START

Go to the
Yoga Studio ↓

Yoga
Studio ↑

FINISH

About the Author

Giselle Shardlow draws from her experiences as a teacher, traveler, mother, and yogi to write her yoga stories for kids. The purpose of her yoga books is to foster happy, healthy, and globally educated children. She lives in Boston with her husband and daughter.

About Kids Yoga Stories

We hope you enjoyed your Kids Yoga Stories experience.
Visit www.kidsyogastories.com to:

Receive updates. For yoga tips, printables, and kids yoga resources, sign up for our free Kids Yoga Stories Newsletter.

Connect with us. Please share with us about your yoga experiences. Send pictures of yourself practicing the poses. Describe your yoga journey on our social media pages (Facebook, Pinterest, Twitter, and Instagram).

Check out free stuff. Read our articles on books, yoga, parenting, and travel. Check out our free kids yoga resources and coloring pages.

Read or write a review. Read what others have to say about our yoga books and kids yoga resources. Post your own review on Amazon or on our website. We would love to hear how you enjoyed these classroom yoga ideas.

Thank you for your support in spreading our message of integrating learning, movement, and fun.

Giselle
Kids Yoga Stories
www.kidsyogastories.com
www.facebook.com/kidsyogastories
www.pinterest.com/kidsyogastories
www.twitter.com/kidsyogastories
www.amazon.com/author/giselleshardlow
www.goodreads.com/giselleshardlow

Yoga Resources by Giselle Shardlow

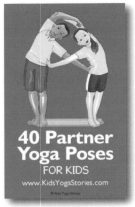

40 Partner Yoga Poses for Kids

Breathing Exercise Cards for Kids

Mindfulness Cards for Kids

Yoga Card Games for Kids

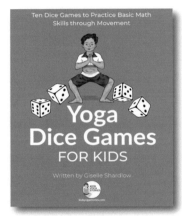

Yoga Dice Games for Kids

"Yogi Says"
and Other Easy Yoga Games

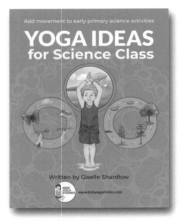

Yoga Ideas for Science Class

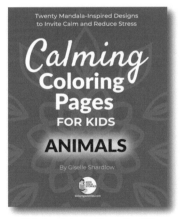

Calming Coloring Pages for Kids

Monthly Kids Yoga Themes

KIDS YOGA STORIES Buy now at www.KidsYogaStories.com/store

Made in the USA
Columbia, SC
05 March 2024